GOD, ANGELS,
AND
DIVINE
INTERVENTION'S

Angel and fallen angel mysteries

W.L. McLaren

xulon
PRESS

www.xulonpress.com

DEDICATION

This book is dedicated to the one true angel I know, my Aunt Sandy, who gave up years of her life to care for her mother, my grandmother. Her years of caring and dedication to her are the basis of what Christianity is.

And to my wonderful wife, Brenda, who is just as unselfish as Sandy and for her dedication to her work in the church.

> *"Let brotherly love continue, be not forgetful to entertain strangers; for thereby some have entertained angels unawares."* (Hebrews 13:1).

TABLE OF CONTENTS

INTRODUCTION

How many times have you heard stories about guardian angels and how they have happened to be in the right place at the right time? They seem to step in at just the right moment in time to save someone from a catastrophic event. We hear about the person who was in an airplane crash and was the sole survivor or the child who was saved when a tornado ripped through a neighborhood and was found untouched in a tree. There was the case of a tornado outbreak in Texas, in which people huddled in a church and prayed and survived. Even though the neighborhood was destroyed, only the church was left untouched.

Yet, the angels are also absent at times. We hear of a child who has been severely abused, and natural disasters where thousands of people are killed or injured. They do not appear to be there, but allow these things to take place. History tells us the terrible atrocities that occurred in the death camps of Auschwitz and Dachau and others; how millions of people suffered terribly and yet, there was no immediate help for them. There was no divine intervention and we can only wonder why. Where was God when the terrible shooting at Columbine High School occurred? I'm sure the people on the Titanic wondered where God was when the loss of life was so high. Every day, these things occur and it appears sometimes divine intervention is there and sometimes it's absent.

I don't think it's wrong to wonder why because those, like myself, are motivated to find out why and try to understand these things. That's the reason I wanted to write this book: to share and research these things and try to understand. I don't claim to have all the answers. I have, however, concluded all things "good or bad" happen for a reason and it's not a coincidence or an accident. It's normal for us to wonder why. I believe the Lord wants to ask questions and even challenge Him on these things in a respectful way, of course.

In my thirty-two years in the Galveston fire department, I had direct knowledge of incidents of angelic intervention and lack thereof. I remember the lady who left her newborn baby at home to go get pizza and returned only to find her house engulfed in flames and her baby dead. I remember the first fire call I made as a rookie where a man died and I saw what fire could do to the human body. I saw people on the worst days of their lives suffering both physical and material losses and I remember wondering why this could happen. When these things happen, we wonder, where's God?

I have also witnessed the opposite, which involved divine intervention and could only be explained as miracles; things that will be talked about in this book that have happened. If I had not witnessed or experienced these things for myself, it would have been difficult to believe. For this, I have no answer other than the fact that angels take their orders from God and He directs their paths. We must keep in mind that angels are there to assist us, but they are also there to make judgments and to stand down in certain situations and allow certain things to happen. If we're going through tough times, it's because it's allowed and it's necessary for us to go through it. They are there to assist us and see us through it, but not to take us out of it. I believe when we find ourselves in a troublesome situation, it's not the situation we should be focusing on, the important thing is how we choose to respond to and handle that situation. How we choose to handle a troublesome situation is our unique opportunity to display our true character and our degree of faith and perseverance. It is here we can evaluate our strengths and weaknesses

I believe angels have certain roles and they are actively involved in God's creation and are constantly assisting both God and His people in their everyday affairs. I believe every person has a guardian angel.

As we get closer to the Lord's return, they will become increasingly active, as we see in the book of Revelation. No other book in the Bible places more emphasis or records more activities of angels than this book.

I would like to share with you the things I have learned about angels through research and some of my own experiences as well as the experiences of others that have had a significant impact on my life and others. I will include facts about angels we often overlook and seldom think about as they play a vital role in God's kingdom and in our everyday walk with the Lord. We will also look at the fallen angels and how they came to where they are now, as well as their functions both past and present. I will present facts that I believe will explain how they were involved with the Great Pyramids and will also point out that God uses both good and bad angels for His purpose. We will also look at the differences between demons and other angels.

As we shall see, angels have a variety of functions and sometimes take on human characteristics such as eating, protecting, and intervening, even appearing as humans. They have a curiosity about us humans and are amazed at the things God does in His everyday affairs with mankind. They witnessed His creation, His birth, His saving work on the cross; they were even involved in healing at times and executing judgment when God instructed them. They don't feel the things we feel except when they take on human form. They have free will, as we have seen in the past when one-third chose to follow Satan and rebel against God. Why they chose to follow Satan and leave their first estate makes one wonder. Jude, the brother of Jesus, wrote in his Epistle, *"and the angels who left their first estate, which kept not their own habitation, he hath reserved in everlasting chains under darkness unto the judgment of the great day.* (Jude 1:6).

Angels at the Door

In my times of need, I often despair
I feel alone and seems nobody cares
That's when I call on my father above
To send me his help, his care and his love
I no sooner plead with my heart even more
It's here I realize the angels are at the door
You cannot see them or touch them so
But they're always around us running to and fro
When I'm down and out, weary and weak.
It's their voice in my head I hear them speak
And remind me of the wonderful love
That's poured down like rain
From our father above
So just when you think you can't take any more
Behold the angels are at the door.

W. McLaren

CHARACTERISTICS OF ANGELS AND FALLEN ANGELS

We cannot begin to understand angels (both good and bad) without knowing their characteristics, what they are like, and what they do. Simply put, angels are spiritual beings created by God to serve Him. He uses evil angels to accomplish things as well. Take, for instance, in the book of Revelation, He uses four angels bound in the Euphrates River to sound the sixth trumpet and are responsible for the war that kills one third of mankind. We know they are evil angels because only evil angels are bound.

The word "angel" in the original translation is *aggelos*, which means, "messenger to bring a message; announces or proclaim."

> *"And the angel said unto them, 'Fear not: for, behold,*
> *I bring you good tidings of great joy, which shall be*
> *to all people.'"* (Luke 2:10).

There are countless numbers of angels. Exactly when they were created is unknown; however, the truth is angels have always existed, just like we have always existed. Now think about this: all of God's creation has always existed, though maybe not in physical form, but in the mind of God. We have always existed, along with His creation. God saw the fall of man in the Garden of Eden, which was the first angelic meeting between humans and an angel. In the eons of time, He saw all human history before it happened.

He saw when you and I were born, grow up, have families, and even knows when and how we will die. He knows who will be saved and who will be damned. Now this is not predestination but rather pre-knowledge. This explains to me why we have moments of déjà vu because things of tomorrow, the next day, or next year have already happened, at least in God's mind,

How many angels there are is unknown. However, it is believed there are as many angels as there are people on earth. There are probably not as many bad angels as there are good angels and this is probably one of the reasons the Nephilim, or the fallen angels, sought to extend themselves through the procreation with human women, which we will discuss.

They were present during the creation of the world and shouted for joy when they witnessed God creating the earth with His creative power.

> *"Whereupon are the foundations thereof fastened? Or who laid the cornerstone thereof; when the morning stars sang together, and all the sons of God shouted for joy?"* (Job 38:6-7)

Please take note that the angels were referred to as the morning stars and the sons of God and we shall address this subject later in this book. Angels have personalities and are highly intelligent, of course. They have emotions and free will like humans do, but unlike humans, they are only spiritual and often appear in the glory of the Lord.

> *"And, lo, the angel of the Lord came upon them, and the glory of the Lord shone round about them: and they were sore and afraid"* (Luke 2:9).

Angels sometimes take on human form as found in Mark 16:5-6: *"and entering the sepulcher, they saw a young man sitting on the right side, clothed in a long white garment; and they were affrighted. And he saith unto them, 'Be not afraid: Ye seek Jesus of*

Nazareth which was crucified: he is risen; he is not here; behold the place where they laid him.

They were there when Jesus ascended into heaven as recorded in the first chapter of Acts:

> *And when he had spoken these things, while they beheld, he was taken up; and a cloud received him out of their sight. and while they looked stead-fastly toward heaven as he went up, behold, two men stood by them in white apparel; which also said, "Ye men of Galilee, why stand ye gazing up into heaven? This same Jesus, which is taken up from you into heaven, shall so come in like manner as ye have seen him go into heaven."* (Acts 1:9-11)

We also see in Genesis 19 two angels appearing as men going into Sodom to rescue Lot right before the Lord destroyed both Sodom and Gomorrah. They also appeared as strange forms as recorded in Isaiah 6 where Isaiah has a vision of God on the throne with angels flying around worshiping Him and in Ezekiel 1. Angels have limitations and are not omniscient (2 Peter 2:11). They also are curious about us and show a desire to learn more about us as the Scriptures indicate: *"Unto whom it was revealed that not unto themselves, but unto us they did minister the things which are now reported unto you by them that have preached the gospel unto you with the Holy Ghost sent down from heaven which things the angels desire to consider"* (1 Peter 1:12).

There are four, possibly six, named angels in the Bible: Michael (also known as the archangel), Gabriel, and one who is known as the angel of the Lord, which some people believe to be the Lord Himself, and, of course, Lucifer. Although I tend not to include Lucifer with these other three, he is considered an angel, albeit the fallen one. His fall from grace is recorded in Isaiah:

> *How art thou fallen from heaven O Lucifer son of the morning? How art thou cut down to the ground, which didst weaken the nations! For thou hast said*

*in thine heart I will exalt my throne above the stars
of God (I am superior to the other angels) I will sit
also sit upon the mount of the congregations in the
sides of the north, I will ascend above the heights
of the clouds: I will be like the most high, yet thou
shall be brought down to hell, to the sides of the pit,
they that see thee shall narrowly look upon thee and
consider thee, saying is this the man that made the
earth tremble. That did shake kingdoms, that made
the world a wilderness, and destroyed the cities
thereof that opened not the house of his prisoners?*
(Isaiah 14:12-17)

Also, the fifth angel mentioned in the Bible is Beelzebub. He is mentioned in Christian demonology as one of the seven princes of hell; it is also, in Arabic, another name for Satan. He is mentioned in the gospels by the Pharisees and the Sadducees when they accused Jesus of casting out demons in his Beelzebub's name.

*"But when the Pharisees heard Jesus was casting out
demons they said this fellow doth not cast devils but
by Beelzebub the prince of devils"* (Matthew 12:24).

Finally, the sixth one is mentioned in the book of Revelation, an angel named Abaddon—or in the original Greek translation, *Apollyon*, which means "destroyer." He is described as the king of an army of locust. It also says he is the angel of the bottomless pit in the book of Revelation. One must wonder if this is the same pit Satan will be confined to.

*And I saw an angel coming down out of heaven
having the key to the bottomless pit and a great
chain in his hand. And he laid hold of the dragon
that old serpent which is the devil and Satan and
bound him a thousand years, and cast him into the
bottomless pit and shut him up and set a seal upon
him that he should deceive the nations no more till*

the thousand years should be fulfilled and after that
he must be loosed a little season. (Revelation 20:1-3)

There are three distinct classifications of angels: cherubim and seraphim, and the fallen angels. The fallen angels are also known as demons and watchers. Seraphim are the highest order of angels, often referred to as the choir angels. Seraphim are attendants or guardians of God's throne. They are seen in Isaiah 6, praising God: *"Above it (God's throne) stood the Seraphim each had six wings; with twain, he covered his face and with twain he covered his feet and with twain he did fly; and one cried unto another and said, 'Holy, Holy, Holy, the whole earth is full of his glory'"* (Isaiah 6:2-3).

The cherub is where Lucifer's rank is and it is second highest in the order. They take on more of a guardian role in the earthly things of God. We see them in the Garden of Eden when Adam and Eve were cast out. Perhaps this is the reason Jesus said Satan was the prince of this world and could explain why he was in the Garden of Eden.

> *"So, he drove out the man and placed him at the east*
> *of the Garden of Eden, cherubim's and a flaming*
> *sword which turned every way to keep the way of*
> *the tree of life"* (Genesis 3:24).

Scripture indicates it was one-third of the cherubim that aligned with Lucifer since he himself is a cherub and joined in his rebellion as seen in the following scripture:

> *Thou hast been in Eden the garden of God: every*
> *precious stone was thy covering, the sardius, the*
> *topaz and the diamond, the beryl, the onyx, and the*
> *jasper, the sapphire, the emerald, and the carbuncle,*
> *and the gold, the workmanship of thy tabrets, and*
> *of thy pipes was prepared in thee in the day thou*
> *were created. Thou art the anointed cherub that*
> *covereth and I have set thee so; thou was upon the*
> *holy mountain of God; thou hast walked up and*

down the midst of the stones of fire. thou was perfect in thy ways from the day thou was created, till iniquity was found in thee. by the multitude of thy merchandise they have filled the midst of thee with violence, and thou hast sinned: therefore will I cast thee out as profane out of the mountain of God; and I will destroy thee, O covering cherub, from the midst of the stones of fire; Thine heart was lifted up because of thy beauty, thou hast corrupted thy wisdom by reason of thy brightness: I will cast thee to the ground, I will lay thee before kings, that they may behold thee. thou hast defiled thy sanctuary by the multitude of thine iniquities, by the iniquity of thy traffic: therefore I will bring forth a fire from the midst of thee, it shall devour thee, and I will bring thee to ashes upon the earth in the sight of all of them that behold thee. and all they that know thee among the people shall be astonished at thee: thou shalt be a terror, and never shalt thou be anymore.
(Ezekiel 28:13-19)

NEPHILIM/ANGEL
CONNECTION

I t is believed, per the book of Enoch, that the cherubim are responsible for the Nephilim/sons of God, as mentioned earlier. The word *Nephilim*, which is translated in the King James Bible, means, "giants," and in the original text is pronounced as *NAPHAL*, which means, "to fall or the fallen ones." The theory is—and this is also recorded in the book of Enoch—these fallen angels or "sons of God" came to earth or descended onto the mountain of Hermon, which, in the Hebrew tongue means "desolation in the land of Jordan," the place of the descent. The rebel angels intended to thwart God's plan for the earth when they were cast down and bred with human women.

These fallen ones sought to merge with the bloodline of Adam and Eve because of the promise to send the Messiah through Adam's descendants. By attempting to destroy the descendants of Adam and Eve, these fallen ones saw the opportunity to extend themselves through humans and afforded an opportunity for Satan to try to prevent the eventual birth of the Messiah. The breeding of human beings and fallen angels, which resulted in these human/angel hybrids, began to corrupt and destroy humanity, resulting in the great flood of Noah's day.

Now, while this is strictly theory and is also recorded in the book of Enoch, it doesn't exactly say this in the Bible. We must assume there must be some truth to it, as evidence would indicate.

I believe the book of Enoch, although it is not one of the original books in the Bible, should be given a lot of credible attention because in the epistle of Jude, it is mentioned and although the book of Enoch was not included in the canon of Scripture, early church historians wrote that the church accepted it as a valid source of information. Therefore, it is plausible to conclude that Jude writing under the inspiration of the Holy Spirit mentions the book of Enoch in his epistle as a valid source of truth.

> *"There were giants in the earth in those days; and after that, when the sons of God came unto the daughters of men, and they bare children unto them, the same became mighty men which were of old, men of renown."* (Genesis 6:4).

The original translation says: *"There were the fallen ones in the earth in those days; and after that, when the sons of God came unto the daughters of men, they bare children unto them, the same became mighty men which were of old, men of renown."* (Genesis 6:4).

Now these children that were produced were a race of giants that once inhabited the earth. We know they existed because in archeological finds, there have been skeletal remains that were anywhere from eight to thirty-six feet tall and they have been found all over the world, meaning they had means of travel.

It is noted these fallen angels/giants instructed their wives and children in all kinds of things, such as new technological skills, magical knowledge, and wisdom on the occult side. This has made it possible to suggest psychic abilities and magical powers were originally an ancient inheritance from the angelic realm given to these early humans. Also, recorded in the book of Enoch, it is stated the leader of these fallen angels was called "Amaze" and he is most closely identified with Lucifer. His name means "light bearer" and Satan. Supposedly, he taught men to forge swords and make shields and body armor. He also taught them metallurgy and how to mine from the earth and use different metals. He taught the women the art of making bracelets, ornaments, rings, and necklaces from precious metals and stones. He also taught them how to beautify their eyelids with cosmetics to seduce the opposite sex. From these practices, according to Enoch, came much godlessness with men and women committing fornication and were led astray, becoming corrupt in their ways. This was the motivation for the early church to condemn the fallen angels for teaching women to make jewelry to wear to church. I believe this is the reason why Pentecostal women do not wear makeup or jewelry in the modern church. The Apostle Paul supports much of what is said here in 1 Corinthians 11:10 in speaking of dress requirements for men and women in church. He admonishes women to cover their heads, *"For this cause, ought the woman to have power on her head because of the angels."*

Many believe this to mean Paul is referencing the fallen angels' attraction to human females with long flowing hair. This custom of women covering their heads in churches is still found today in Roman Catholicism and the customs of Islam.

STRANGE CONNECTION BETWEEN FALLEN ANGELS AND THE PYRAMIDS OF EGYPT

A t first, I found these things strange and hard to believe. Then, during my research, I began to focus my attention on the things recorded in the book of Enoch about the fallen angels instructing humanity on technological things and my mind went immediately to the mysteries of the pyramids. There has always been a question as to who built them and why. So, when I read fallen angels left their heavenly realm and came here and instructed humankind according to the book of Enoch, it was like a light switch went off in my head, so I started looking at the pyramids and all the facts that surround them. I personally believe it was these fallen ones who built the pyramids and, in fact, they are the only ones that could have, when you look at the facts and the mysteries surrounding the pyramids. I think it raises a lot of circumstantial evidence to this theory. So, let's look at some facts on the pyramids of Egypt.

1. The pyramid is estimated to have 2,300,000 stone blocks weighing two to thirty tons each and there are some blocks that weigh over fifty tons. How these blocks were transported and assembled into the pyramid is still a mystery; it would be humanly impossible for these pyramids to be built by humans. It would take millions and millions of manpower and hundreds of years. However, an army of giants, some thirty-six feet tall with advanced technology, could do it easily.

2. The pyramid of Menkaure, the pyramid of Khafre, and the great pyramid of Khufu are precisely aligned with the constellation of Orion.

3. The cornerstone foundations of the pyramids have ball and socket construction, capable of dealing with heat expansion and earthquakes.

4. The mortar used is of an unknown origin. It has been analyzed and its chemical composition is known, but cannot be reproduced. It is stronger than the stone and is still holding up today.

5. The outer mantle was composed of 144,000 casing stones, all of them highly polished and flat to an accuracy of 1/100th of an inch, about 100 inches thick and weighing approximately fifteen tons each.

   *This raised a red flag for me and as of now, I cannot make the connection, but in the book of Revelation, there is a vision John saw of an angel ascending out of the east, instructing the four angels of the Euphrates saying, *"Hurt not the earth, neither the sea, nor the trees, till we have sealed the servants of our God in their foreheads. and I heard the number of them which were sealed: and there* *were sealed a hundred and forty and four thousand of all the tribes of the children of Israel"* (Revelation 7:2-4). There may not be any connection, but I found it strange that these casing stones were the same number of the sealed servants in the book of Revelation, which are the twelve tribes of Israel.

6. The pyramids were originally covered in casing stones made of highly polished limestone. These casing stones reflected the sun's light and made the pyramids shine like a jewel. It has been calculated that at one time, they could act as a gigantic mirror and reflect light so powerful that it would be visible from the moon as a shining star on earth.

7. The interior temperature is constant and equals the average temperature of the earth, about sixty-eight degrees Fahrenheit.

8. The Great Pyramid is located at the exact center of the land mass of the earth, the east/west parallel that crosses the most land and the north/south meridian that crosses the most land intersect in two places: one in the ocean and the other at the Great Pyramid. In short, the Great Pyramid is positioned exactly at the latitude and longitude lines that contain more land and sea mass than any other place on earth and it's right in the geographical center of the earth. This fact alone implies that the builders knew a great deal about the geography of our planet. It's hard to imagine they could accomplish this without an aerial view. So, we must ask ourselves, how was this accomplished?

9. There's a granite coffer in the king's chamber that's too big to fit through the passages, so it must have been put in place during construction. The purpose of this coffer is unknown, but it is made from solid granite and looks like a cement block that caskets are encased in to keep the casket from rising above ground during torrential flooding. It was cut from a block of granite and would require bronze saws with eight to nine-foot-long sets of teeth made of sapphires. Hollowing out the interior of the coffer would require tubular drills of the same material, applied with

a tremendous vertical force. Microscopic analysis of the coffer reveals it was made with a fixed-point drill that used hard jewel bits and a drilling force of two tons.

10. The centers of the four sides are indented with an extraordinary degree of precision, forming what looks like eight sides. This effect is not visible from the ground or from a distance, but only from the air, and only under the proper lighting conditions and the dawn and sunset on the spring and autumn equinoxes and when the sun casts shadows on the pyramids.

11. The Great Pyramid (Ikhet) had a swivel door entrance at one time. Swivel doors were found in only two other pyramids. It has been reported that when the pyramid was first opened that the swivel door, weighing twenty tons, was so well balanced that it could be opened by pushing out from the inside with only minimal force. When it was closed, it was such a perfect fit, it could barely be detected and there wasn't enough of a crack or crevice around the edges to gain a grip from the outside to open it.

12. The pyramids had or has a connection with outer space; the descending passage pointed to the pole star Alpha Dacronis. It is estimated in 2170-2144 BC, this was the North Star at that point in time. No other star has aligned with the passage since then. The southern shaft in the king's chamber pointed to the constellation Orion, circa 2450 BC. The Orion constellation was associated with the Egyptian god, Osiris. No other star aligned with this shaft during that time in history.

13. The overall precision of the Great Pyramid is astonishing. It's 750 feet long at each base, situated along the four cardinal points: north, south, east, and west. The ratio of its circumference to its original height is equal to the value of pi: 3.14. This is not supposed to have been known for at least another 1,000 years. The mathematical and astronomical knowledge that were applied to the pyramids are a great mystery to modern day scholars.

I didn't mean to go in depth about the pyramids, but I want to make the connection between these great structures and the fallen angels. The book of Enoch records these beings did come down to earth and did mate with human females, as recorded in Genesis 6, and they did instruct humans on many different technological methods and exposed them to things many years ahead of their time, such as metallurgy and how to mine the earth and use different metals.

There are many different archaeological structures all over the world that were built with no explanation, and the Great Pyramids are no exception. The modern theories that are taught say humans built them as a burial place for the pharaohs, even though professional Egyptologists have dismissed these claims numerous times. The pyramids contain so many facts and mysteries that remain unanswered to this day; just the fact that they were built all over the planet at different time periods by civilizations that had no contact with one another is enough to raise eyebrows.

If you believe the theory that humans built these mysterious structures as nothing more than a tomb for the pharaohs and completely rule out the evidence of the fallen angels coming down to earth and teaching human's technological methods centuries ahead of their time and possibly building the pyramids themselves, then consider the following:

Over two million blocks of stone were used to build the pyramid that covers more than thirteen acres of land (thirteen being the number of the illuminati; again, not sure of the connection). It's also estimated between 2.3 and 2.6 million blocks of stone were used to build the Great Pyramid. It originally had outer casings of limestone blocks that were perfectly polished and fitted for thousands of years. It shined like a gleaming structure like no other and it must be remembered we're talking about structures that were built around 10500 BC and 3500 BC. Erosion and elements of the weather are what we see today. What power could have moved these stones?

Think about these 2.5 million stones that weigh between two and twenty tons each that were cut with laser-like precision with tools that are not even replicated today and how they were fitted perfectly in place. How did they lift and transport them from their original position across the terrain, desert, water, and sand and then lift them on top of each other to build the pyramids? Even if the workers achieved the impossible feat of ten blocks piled on top of each other a day, they would have assembled the 2.5 million stone blocks into the stone pyramid in about 250,000 days or 664 years, not even long enough for the one it was supposedly built for to see its completion. It would be impossible for a group of enough men to lift a stone that's three and one half feet high and three and one half feet long that weighs about 9,000 pounds off a barge and then maneuver it in place on the pyramid. Even if it were possible, it would take ten men, three on one side and two on each end. This placement would be lifting 900 pounds. This display of strength would be difficult for a normal man, but not a man upward of twelve to thirty-six feet. Considering all these facts in human terms, it would require the use of millions of people and at that time in history, there were not that many people on earth. There would have had to be a large population of engineers, mathematicians, farmers, merchants, an army of slaves, and many more involved. The fallen ones coming down to the earth is recorded in the book of Revelation, which I believe is currently being played out now and not a future event. The reason I believe this is because the book of Revelation is not written in chronological order and is an overall picture of the story of creation from the beginning to the end. It gives us insight into the past, present, and future. When John wrote this masterpiece, he was told by Jesus to *"Write the things which thou have seen, the things which are, and the things which shall be hear after;"* (Revelation 1:19).

Satan's goal in organizing the Nephilim/human hybridization program was to corrupt the bloodline that would eventually pro-duce Jesus Christ, the Messiah and the Redeemer of mankind. God saw this as evil and decided to destroy the world with the great Flood of Noah's day. Now that the end times are upon us, we see Satan switching tactics and once again attempting to manip-ulate human beings on a grand scale by way of human genetics by increasing the population of homosexuals, transsexuals, trans-gender, and every kind of sexual perversion imaginable—only, this time, it is not the prevention of the coming of the Messiah, but to prevent any flesh from being saved. In Matthew 24:37, Jesus is giving His apostles some signs to look for in the end times and He makes this astonishing statement: *"But as the days of Noah were, so shall also the coming of the son of man be."* In other words, Jesus said in the last days it would be exactly the way it was in the days of Noah. This statement brings up an important question: could we possibly see the same thing happening in these last days that happened in the days of Noah?

In Numbers 13, the Israelis scouted out the land of Canaan so they sent out some spies to check it out. When they came back, the report was not good. Their enemies, the Amalekites, were in the land of the south while the Hittites, the Jebusites, and the Amorites were in the mountains; the Canaanites were by the sea. Yet, their worst problem was the giants (or fallen ones) were in the land once again.

> *And they brought up an evil report of the land which they reported unto the children of Israel saying, the land, though which we have gone to search it, is a land that eateth up its inhabitants thereof; and all the people that we saw in it are men of a great stature. And we saw the giants, (fallen ones), the sons of Anak which come of the giants: and we were in our own sight as grasshoppers, and so we were in their sight.* (Numbers 13:32-33)

Now this brings up all kinds of issues that must be addressed. One fact we must not overlook is that the fallen ones somehow continued their efforts after the flood and once again were present on the earth, procreating with women and corrupting the bloodline of mankind. The Bible records they were all destroyed, so this brings up some debatable questions.

How did the giants appear once again on earth after the Bible says they were destroyed?

Why would God allow this to happen again after He destroyed them for doing the same thing?

They are not mentioned again in the Bible, so where did they go? What happened to them? Are they still among us?

While thinking about this, I came up with a possible answer to the first question of how they survived the great Flood. Since the Bible clearly says they were all destroyed outside the ark, the only conclusion I can humanly think of is their genes were carried over on Noah's ark, possibly by one of Noah's sons or daughters-in-law. There's indication it was Ham or his wife. shortly after the Flood subsided. Noah had planted a vineyard and drank the wine and had gotten drunk. Then there was an incident in which Ham's son, Canaan, did something to Noah and Canaan was cursed for it. We do not know exactly what it was, but we are given certain clues from Scripture from the original translation.

> *And he drank of the wine, of the vineyard and was drunken; and was uncovered within his tent. and Ham, the father of Canaan, saw the nakedness of his father, and told his two brethren without. and Shem and Japheth took a garment, and laid it upon both their shoulders, and went backward, and covered the nakedness of their father; and their faces were backward and they saw not their father's nakedness. and Noah awoke from his wine, and knew what his younger son had done unto him. and he said, "Cursed be Canaan; a servant of servants shall he be unto his brethren."* (Genesis 9:21-25)

The Hebrew word for nakedness, *erwah*, means, "shameful nakedness" and is often used as immoral behavior. For simple nakedness or bareness, the word used is *eyrom*, so we have a clear indication here that an immoral act was done to Noah substantiating the fact that the sins of the people that were destroyed in the flood were carried aboard the ark by his grandson whose seed would later manifest itself in the Canaanite people who were known to practice all kinds of wickedness, including child sacrifices. This also is the land where the Israeli spies would later report that there were giants in the land where they dwelt (Numbers 13:33).

AS IN THE DAYS OF NOAH

It was recorded that these giants or fallen angels were so huge that normal men, compared to them, were like grasshoppers. Now there's a popular theory that when the Nephilim came down, they came down as extraterrestrials and there are some ancient hieroglyphics in Egypt depicting men in some sort of astronaut suit, taken with the fact that Jesus said in the last days it would *"be exactly as it was in the days of Noah."*

Now if you take this literally, then we would be looking at certain circumstances that happened in the days of Noah and things that are similarly happening today. Now let's look at what was going on in the days of Noah and what's happening today and compare the two.

1. In the days of Noah, there was a small group of people in the last days before the Flood, warning people of the coming tribulation and calamity.

2. The main theme before Noah's day was the interaction of fallen angels and human beings in Genesis 6. The offspring that was produced from the procreation of fallen angels and human women produced the Nephilim and they were present in the world. Recently, on the radio show "Coast to Coast" with Steve Qualye, he shared a story from the website, "Just another WordPress.com" in November 2009. He received a call from a pilot friend who gave an account of some cargo he transported from Afghanistan to an unknown destination. It was a corpse of a twelve-foot man

who weighed about 1,500 pounds. He went on to describe him as having six fingers and six toes. This twelve-foot giant had attacked a small squadron who had ventured into the mountains of Afghanistan in search of the Taliban. Nine soldiers were ripped apart and eaten before it was killed. They reported it was capable of running at incredible speeds and was strong in both strength and smell. This size would be considered minor compared to the thirty-foot skeletal remains that have been unearthed; twelve feet tall would put him as being the same size as biblical Goliath. So according to this story, the Nephilim/giants are once again on the earth, just like in the days of Noah and just like Jesus said it would be. If we are truly living in the end times, then we should be looking for the fallen angels to once again manifest themselves on earth in the form of superior or extraterrestrial beings. Given advanced technology Jesus said in Matthew 24 that "knowledge shall be increased" in the end times as in the days of Noah, these fallen angels will look to oversee a breeding program involving human beings. Now whether alien abduction is true or a fabricated lie, a few things are constant: the women all reported the aliens experimenting on their female reproductive organs and the men reported semen being extracted from them. The manifestation of fallen angels in Noah's day also contributed to widespread paganism, rebellion, violence, and occultism and widespread sexual perversion. It's not hard to look at the world we live in today and see we are living as it was in the days of Noah.

In the *Hagmann Report*, dated May 25, 2016, Project Chimera: The Beast of Old Return, Scientists Creating Human & Animal Hybrids, we talk of the giants and individuals will assume one is "off their rocker," but talk of scientists creating animal and human hybrids, everyone is in belief. It's called Chimera, and it's the latest project regarding human and animal hybrids. The ethic boundaries prohibit the interbreeding of mankind and animals. However, science has done just that. Scientists are attempting not to create a human animal hybrid, but rather, recreate it. The researchers are attempting to grow tissue inside of pigs and sheep with the goal of creating of hearts, livers, or other organs needed for transplants. The people of the world understand this is not for the benefit of medicine; rather, it is to further the agenda and recreate the beast of old. The Nephilim still exists, and it is believed these creatures still walk among us, look like us, talk like us, and act like us. However, under their skin, they are the world's worst nightmare. The things that should not be are making their return beginning with our physical structure, DNA. Scientists are attempting to blur the lines between species. Mixing animals and humans is not a small task and it is highly unacceptable. Where does science stop? That's the real question. So far, scientists can alter DNA to unwilling individuals through GMOs (Genetically Modified Organisms) and now, just as in the days of Noah, so shall it be also in the days of the son of man.

The thought has recently come to me that this could also explain all the sightings of the Sasquatch or Bigfoot. There has never been any physical evidence of a Bigfoot except for some footprints casting. Still, there have been sightings. Maybe Bigfoot or Sasquatch is a by-product of these experiments. Some believe it's possible they are spiritual and are inter-dimensional, meaning they can travel in and out of our dimension. This could explain why they have never been captured, nor has there ever been any skeletal remains. I'll let you draw your own conclusions on these theories.

I must also mention here that in the *Book of Giants* found with the Dead Sea Scrolls, it is recorded these giants not only mated with human women, but also animals, which makes the mystery of Bigfoot even more intriguing. Could they be a leftover remnant of these hybrid beings? Again, you can draw your own conclusions. Just the saying that they came down to earth means they were above us and came out of the sky. There's a popular theory that suggest that these fallen angels in the last days will perpetrate themselves as alien beings that return to earth and manifest themselves to humans and will bring great or more knowledge to us. Maybe even the antichrist himself will come as an alien and present "great signs and wonders" and will deceive many people just as Jesus said, it would.

> *There shall be signs in the sun, and in the moon, and in the stars; and upon the earth distress of nations, with perplexity; the sea and the waves roaring; (it would be so fearful) that men's hearts would be failing them for fear, and for looking after those things which are coming on the earth: for the powers of heaven shall be shaken.* (Luke 21:25-26)

The Bible gives us hints of these fallen angels dwelling in the sky. Listen to the Apostle Paul in his letter to the Ephesians: *"For we wrestle not against flesh and blood, but against principalities, against powers, against the rulers of the darkness of this world, against spiritual wickedness in high places."* (Ephesians 6:12).

WHAT ANGELS DO

As I stated in the introduction, angels are spiritual beings that worship God and are actively involved with the everyday affairs, assisting God and us. They worship the Lord and serve Him through various means and situations. In Isaiah, we see the seraphim flying high above the throne of God, worshiping and even having a part in commissioning Isaiah to his earthly ministry.

> *"I saw also the Lord sitting on his throne, high and lifted up, and his train filled the temple. above it stood the Seraphim's; each one had six wings; with twain he covered his face, and with twain he covered his feet, he did fly. and one cried, unto another, and said, 'Holy, Holy, Holy, is the Lord of host: the whole earth is full of his glory.'"* (Isaiah 6:1-3).

He sometimes empowers them with great power to execute judgment on God's commands; such was the case in 2 Samuel 24. King David had ordered a census be taken of the people and the anger of the Lord was kindled against David. Now there are a few different held beliefs why this angered the Lord so much. Most scholars believe, however, that King David was eaten up with pride and arrogance; plus, it was another way to tax the people even more. Whatever the case, God gave him a choice of punishment: seven years of famine, three months running from his enemies, or three days of pestilence in the land. David chose the latter. So, the Lord sent a pestilence upon Israel from the morning until the appointed time and Scripture tells us 70,000 people died from this pestilence.

> *"And when the angel stretched out his hand upon Jerusalem to destroy it, the Lord repented him of the evil, and said to the angel that destroyed the people, 'It is enough: stay now thy hand. and the angel of the Lord was by the threshing place of Araunah the Jebusite'"* (2 Samuel 24:16).

We also see in the Old Testament the Lord providing an angel to escort the children of Israel, not only showing them the way, but also empowering him with tremendous power, even the power to forgive transgressions to direct their paths in every step.

> *Behold, I send an angel before thee, to keep in the way, and to bring thee into the place which I have prepared. Beware of him, and obey his voice, provoke him not: for he will not pardon your transgressions: for my name is in him. But if thou wilt indeed obey his voice, and do all that I speak; then I will be an enemy to thine enemies, and an adversary to your adversaries. For mine angel, shall go before thee, and bring thee unto the Amorites, the Hittites, and the Perizzites, and the Canaanites, the Hivites, and the Jebusites: and I will cut them off.* (Exodus 23:20-23)

Angels are directly involved in bringing answers to prayer requests. In Daniel 10, Daniel had trouble with a vision he had seen and was in deep prayer to understand when an angel was sent to him to assist him with his prayer request.

> *And he said unto me, "Oh Daniel, a man greatly beloved, understand the words that I speak unto thee, and stand upright: for unto thee am I now sent.*

> *And when he had spoken this word unto me, I stood*
> *trembling. Then said he unto me, 'Fear not, Daniel:*
> *for from the first day that thou didst set Thine heart*
> *to understand, and chasten thyself before God, thy*
> *words were heard, and I have come for thy words.'"*
> (Daniel 10:11-12)

Angels observe and are curious about our world: "*Unto whom it was revealed, that not unto themselves, but unto us they did minister the things, which are now reported unto you by them that have preached the gospel unto you with the Holy Ghost sent down from heaven; which things the angels desire to look into.*" (1 Peter 1:12)

They were there at the birth of Jesus and even participated in the announcement:

> *And suddenly there was with the angel a multi-*
> *tude of the heavenly host praising God, and saying,*
> *"Glory to God in the highest, and on earth peace,*
> *and goodwill toward men." And it came to pass, as*
> *the angels were gone away from them into heaven,*
> *the shepherds said one to another, "Let us now go*
> *even unto Bethlehem, and see this thing which is*
> *come to pass, which the Lord hath made known*
> *unto us." (Luke 2:13-15)*

As we see here, angels have access to earth and heaven and it is confirmed in several Bible verses, such as the dream of Jacob at Bethel. "*And he dreamed, and behold a ladder set up on the earth, and the top of it reached to heaven: and behold the angels of God ascending and descending on it*" (Genesis 28:12).

No doubt they were amazed when the Son of God came to earth to start His ministry as we see them in the wilderness witnessing the temptation of Jesus. They were evidently ordered to stand down while the Lord underwent His three temptations. Afterward, we know they came and ministered to Him: "*Then the devil leaveth him, and behold, angels came and ministered unto him*" (Matthew 4:11).

I'm sure they were heartbroken when they saw His work on the cross and probably did not understand the very Son of God was subjected to the total and absolute degradation of "he who knew no sin." I'm sure they could not justify the fact in their minds that the Father allowed this to happen and they were not to interfere, but to merely stand by and let it run its course. One can only imagine what words of encouragement were given to Jesus by way of an angel dispatched from heaven to meet Jesus in the garden when Jesus prayed and asked if there was not another way to accomplish His great task.

> *"And there appeared an angel from heaven, strength-*
> *ening him"* (Luke 22:43).

ANGELS ARE PROTECTORS

To most people, particularly unbelievers, Jesus suffered a humiliating defeat in His ministry, all the way from His early days preaching in the synagogues to His tragic and dreadful day on the cross. Yet, nothing could be further from the truth. Jesus was in total control the whole time and willingly allowed Himself to be subject to things that He surely did not deserve. He could have stopped it anytime and called on heavenly reinforcements and saved Himself. He made this perfectly clear in the Garden of Gethsemane when one who was with Jesus (presumably Peter), drew a sword and smote a servant of the high priest and cut off his ear. In rebuking him, Jesus made the statement: *"Put up again thy sword unto its place: for all that take up the sword shall parish with the sword. Thinkest thou that I cannot not now pray to my Father, and he shall presently give me more than twelve legions of angels? But how then shall the scriptures be fulfilled, that thus it must be?"* (Matthew 26:52-56).

There's no doubt from this Scripture Jesus had total control over His situation and could have stopped it any time. Yet, He was determined to carry out the Father's will. Angels were available and willing in the event they were called upon to provide protection upon hearing the request, but in this case, that request never came. Angels in the New Testament actively protected the apostles and sometimes they were not, as they actively established the Lord's church, much to the displeasure of the religious leaders of that day. They were heavily persecuted; they were constantly threatened, sometimes beaten, sometimes thrown into prison. Eventually all, except the Apostle John, would suffer a terrible death.

One incident we see in the book of Acts. We see an angel assisting Peter. As the story goes, Herod had killed James, the brother of John, because it pleased the Jews of that day. Seeing this, he apprehended Peter and had him thrown into prison. Later that evening, Herod sought to bring forth Peter whose hands and feet were bound between two soldiers. Then an angel appears with a bright light and had to wake up Peter. The Scripture says:

> *The angel smote peter on the side, and raised him up saying, "Arise up quickly." and his chains fell from his hands. and the angel said unto him, "Gird thyself, and bind on thy sandals." and so he did. and he saith unto him, "Cast thy garment about thee, and follow me." and he went out, and followed him; and wist not that it was true which was done by the angel; but thought he saw a vision. When they were past the first and second ward, they came unto the iron gate that leadeth unto the city; which opened to them of their own accord; and they went out, and passed through one street; and forthwith the angel departed from him.* (Acts 12:7-10)

Also in Acts, we see an angel dealing out a punishing judgment on Herod the king. To set the stage on this story, Herod had been persecuting the apostles, but was thwarted by God on several occasions, such as the angel releasing Peter from prison. In his rebellion and anger toward God because he was the king and wasn't about to share his kingdom with anyone, he set aside a special day for himself to defy God.

> *And upon a set day Herod, arrayed in royal apparel, sat upon his throne, and made an oration unto them. and the people (out of fear of him) gave a shout, saying, "It is the voice of a god and not of a man." (implying that Herod was more than a man and*

*he was in the status of a god) and immediately the
angel of the Lord smote him, because he gave not
God the glory: and he was eaten of worms, and
gave up the ghost. but the word of God grew and
multiplied.* (Acts 12:21-24)

I have come to believe the reason the angels weren't always
there to protect the Christians in the early days of the church was
because the church flourishes when there's persecution. I'm sure
the angels were frustrated when they had to stand by and watch
when Christians were slaughtered in Nero's circus. Some were
killed by wild animals. Some were burned alive and used as street-
lights. When Satan tried to destroy the church by violence, it only
brought about increases. It was to be in his mind that through violence, he would destroy the church, but through persecution, he
only helped increase the church. The more persecution he inflicted
or should I say, could inflict, the more the church grew. God used
Satan to build the church, the very thing he tried to destroy. We
should admire the faith and courage the early church had and the
perseverance to endure the sufferings they experienced for the Lord.

DIVINE INTERVENTION IN WORLD WAR II

One of the most famous stories of divine intervention occurred during World War II and it's called "The Miracle of Dunkirk." This is the story of how 300,000 British troops were snatched from the beaches of France that it can only be called a miracle. It was May 1940, a time dark and dangerous for the British Empire and the entire civilized world. Hitler had launched his *blitzkrieg* against France and the surrounding countries. By the second week of May, the French forces were broken. Rommel and his seventh panzer division, with lightning speed, had broken through and advanced across France and Belgium. It wasn't long until Rommel's armored pincher movement threatened the British army with encirclement and the only option they had was to evacuate. However, the problem was where to evacuate, as they were backed against the English Channel with nowhere to go. This put Winston Churchill in the position of fearing he possibly was facing the greatest military disaster in history and it would be his responsibility to publicly announce this difficult news to the people of England.

On May 25th, even the German high command had boasted on the fact that "the British army is surrounded and our troops are on the verge of annihilating them." With the situation rapidly deteriorating, the decision was made back in England to evacuate as many as possible and with some luck, they might be able to get at least 20,000 or 30,000 men at best, but the problem with that was the only port they could possibly do this from was Dunkirk, which was threatened by the Germans.

The outlook was bleak. Either the entire—or at least, most—of the British forces were about to be annihilated and perish, or be taken prisoner and starved to death in captivity. Then there would be nothing left to stop Hitler from conquering all of Europe. Everything appeared to be lost.

Upon hearing and seeing this developing situation, King George VI requested Sunday, May 26th should be observed as a National Day of Prayer. In a radio broadcast, he called on the people of the British Empire to commit their cause to God. The king, along with members of his cabinet, visited Westminster Abbey, along with millions of Britain's flocking to churches to join in prayer. Photographs of Westminster Abbey and other churches showed long lines of people, some not even being able to get in. The whole nation was in prayer. The following morning, the daily newspaper exclaimed, "Nothing like this has ever happened before" with the country being united in prayer in their hour of deep distress. These heartfelt prayers went up to God and by no means went unanswered. What was to follow was not one miracle, but a series of miracles (God is not limited when it comes to miracles). The first miracle that happened, which, to this day has never been explained or understood, is just when a massive military victory was in Hitler's hands and the door opened for Hitler to have access to all of Europe, for an unexplained reason, Hitler ordered a halt to all operations and ordered his top generals back to headquarters in Berlin. Some believe Hitler pondered using his air superiority to annihilate the British and that this would be sufficient to prevent a large-scale evacuation by sea. This was a crucial factor in terms of the second miracle.

The second miracle came in the form of an unprecedented storm with great fury, which broke out over the region on Tuesday, May 28, grounding the German Luftwaffe (air force), enabling the British troops to make their way to the beach under the cover of darkness and the violence of the storm and the rain without any fear of being bombed from above from the grounded German planes, which could not operate in such turbulent conditions. Hitler did not take into consideration He who controls the weather. Despite the unprecedented and turbulent storm grounding the German war planes, a great calm such as rarely been experienced settled over the English Channel and could only be described as "being as still as a mill pond." It was this quite extraordinary calm which made it possible for a vast armada of both privately owned fishing boats, little ships, big ships, war ships, and anything that could float to be able to travel back and forth in the English Channel in a desperate attempt to rescue as many men as possible. There were so many boats of all sizes that one described it as a huge traffic jam going back and forth in the English Channel and that one could walk across the English Channel from one side to the other on the decks of the boat without even getting their feet wet. This miracle not only saved thousands of lives, but also prevented Hitler from possibly conquering all of Europe and enabled the British to reorganize their troops and eventually to join the allies later to help defeat Hitler.

ANGELIC INTERVENTION IN THE HOLY LAND

Angelic intervention in the Holy Land is nothing new and I have recently had the opportunity to hear firsthand of accounts of angelic protection in the land that God chose to put His name. We had the privilege of having Gershon Solomon of the Temple Mount Faithful speak at our church. Now the Temple Mount Faithful is an organization that is dedicated to the rebuilding of the temple in Israel, which the Bible tells us will be rebuilt in the end times. Gershon Solomon is their main speaker who travels all over the world, raising money for this effort. I had a one-on-one conversation with him and he told me a remarkable story of angelic intervention, one of which had happened to him while serving in the Israeli Defense Forces during the six-day war, also known as the 1967 war.

The incident took place when Gershon found himself separated from his unit, wounded and lost. He had tried to hide in a hole when a group of Arabs found him, surrounded him with their weapons loaded and ready to fire and kill him on the spot. He braced himself, ready to face death, when suddenly they started frantically speaking in Arabic and rapidly left the scene without firing a shot. Gershon would eventually be rescued by some IDF soldiers. Later, Gershon would find out that some of the Arabs were captured and when being questioned and asked why they suddenly abandoned what would have been an easy kill of an Israeli soldier, their response was they were terrified of the giants that were on the hills armed with huge swords which could only be explained as angelic beings.

Another story I remember reading about was a unit of the IDF found themselves in a terrible predicament in the 1973 Yom Kippur War, as they were in an intense confrontation with the Syrian army. Commander David Yinni was in the process of pulling his troops out of this confrontation when they realized they were trapped in a minefield. Knowing it would take a miracle for them to make it out alive, the troops began crawling on their bellies while using their bayonets to try to dig in the dirt to find the mines without setting them off. At some point, one of the soldiers decided to utter a heartfelt prayer. As the story goes, suddenly, a windstorm blew in. The soldiers hunkered down until the storm subsided, feeling somewhat protected as the dust in the wind concealed their location for the time being. When the storm subsided, it had blown away so much of the dirt that the mines were exposed and the entire platoon managed to escape unharmed. This is known as the "Yom Kippur miracle."

MISSILES ARE NO MATCH

A t the writing of this book, Israel is once again embroiled in a military campaign against the Hamas terrorist group that has been firing thousands of rockets into Israel, fortunately with little damage or loss of life; thanks, of course, to divine protection. In some cases, the Lord Himself directly intervenes as it appears here. In one of three incidents of divine protection comes a story in a world net daily article dated august 5th 2014, of an operator of Israel's Iron Dome Missile Defense System, who said he personally witnessed "the hand of God" diverting an incoming rocket out of harm's way. The commander stated a missile was fired from Gaza and an iron dome precisely calculated the trajectory of the missile. They know where these missiles will land: down to a radius of about 200 meters. He said this missile was projected to hit either the Kara Towers (Israel's equivalent to the Pentagon of the United States) or a central Tel Aviv railway station, where hundreds could have been killed.

When we fired the first interceptor missile; it missed. We fired a second interceptor missile; it missed, which is extremely rare. I was in shock; at this point, we had just four seconds until the missile would land. We had already notified emergency services to converge on the target location and warned of a mass-casualty incident. Suddenly, iron dome (which calculates wind speeds, among other things) showed a major wind coming from the east that was so strong that it sent the missile into the sea. We were all stunned. I stood up and shouted, "There is a God."

The commander went on to say, "I witnessed this miracle with my own eyes; it was not told me or reported to me. I saw the hand of God send that missile into the sea."

There is no doubt there this was divine intervention here. One terrorist was asked why they couldn't aim their rockets more effectively to which he stated, "We do but their God changes their paths in midair."

Former Prime Minister David Ben Gurion stated, "In Israel, to be a realist, you must believe in miracles."

A DOVE IN HAND

On August 5, 2014, an Israeli soldier returning from the Gaza campaign shared a strange story in a synagogue with a prominent Jewish rabbi's wife. She posted on her official Facebook page of an incident that took place with his unit involving a miracle dove. His army unit had identified the home of a Hamas terrorist. They arrived undercover early one morning at the house and were about to enter when they noticed a dove hovering overhead. They paused for a second to watch the dove land on a piece of string. A second later, the entire house blew up. The house was booby trapped and the string was connected to the door. If the soldiers had entered the house, they would have been killed.

God sends His angels in all different shapes and sizes to protect His people. Praise God for His intervention in using this little sweet dove.

> After reading these stories, there's one verse that comes to mind: *"Yea, though I walk through the shadow of death, I will fear no evil: for thou art with me; thy rod and thy staff they comfort me."* (Psalm 23).

HE COMETH IN THE CLOUDS

On August 6, 2014, during the Gaza operation, Givati brigade commander Colonel Ofer Winter gave an interesting account to the weekly publication, *Mishpacha*. He stated he had witnessed a miraculous occurrence, the likes of which he had never seen before during his military career. Winter indicated a predawn raid intended to use darkness as a delay, forcing the soldiers to move toward their objective as sunrise approached. With the troops in danger of being exposed at daybreak, Winter explained how a heavy fog quickly descended to shroud their movements until their mission was accomplished.

"Suddenly a cloud protected us," he said, referring to the clouds in the Bible that guided the ancient Israelites as they wondered in the desert, "clouds of glory."

Winters went on to say only when they were in a secure position did the fog finally lift.

> *"For the Lord your God is the he that who goes with you, to fight for you against your enemies, to save you."* (Deuteronomy 20:4).

THE BUTTERFLY PEOPLE OF JOPLIN, MISSOURI

On Sunday, May 22, 2011, Joplin, Missouri was about to experience a catastrophe. To understand what happened here, you must get the full picture of what these people experienced in a Midwestern town of 50,000 people. Before the day was over, they would have been to hell and back. A tornado outbreak was about to occur that would leave a path of death and destruction that they would never forget. The tornado killed 161 people. It wiped out entire neighborhoods with more than 900 houses destroyed and large stores collapsed into piles of rubble. The landscape wasn't even recognizable.

I can relate, after all the storms that I had experienced. Still, there was something else the tornado released: stories about death and unlikely survival. A teenager was sucked from a SUV. A toddler was plucked from his mother's arms. Houses exploded from 200mph winds as families huddled together in closets and bathtubs. For months afterward, when people assembled together, especially children, they would share stories about being saved by something nothing short of a miracle and they all had one thing in common with each other. They would come to describe being saved by what they called "the butterfly people." I call them angels.

One of the most famous stories of these butterfly people is the story of a two-and-a-half-year-old girl who, with her father, was caught in the tornado in their vehicle. Afterward, she was encouraged to tell of her experience (for therapeutic reasons, to release any fears or anxiety she may have been possessing), so she began to tell this amazing story. She said she and her dad and the butterfly people were in the car.

It was at this point that she was interrupted by her dad and told that it was just him and her in the car, but she insisted, "No, Daddy, there were butterfly people in the car with us."

Now, isn't that amazing? This child would not normally know what an angel was so she was describing them as something she was familiar with, which were butterflies.

Another similar story was a young boy and his father was also in their vehicle and being tossed and thrown about wildly in the wind. Suddenly, the father looked up to see another car flying right toward them. The little boy would go on to say later that two large angels or butterfly people held the other car back and their car was never hit by this other car. The boy was adamant it was two large angels that held the car back. He was the only one who saw them. The father witnessed the miracle, but the child was the only one who saw who was responsible for this miracle.

In another incredible story of divine intervention, a sheriff's deputy patrolled the area immediately following the storm when he spotted a four-year-old boy sitting in an open field east of Joplin. The deputy ran to get him, thinking he needed medical attention, when he noticed there wasn't a scratch on him. He asked the little boy where he lived, which was west Joplin near the St. John's Hospital, which took a horrific hit.

The deputy asked him how he got to this field and the boy replied, "The angels brought me and set me down here."

The distance was more than three miles from where he was picked up.

A mother and her young daughter were in their vehicle when they saw the tornado coming toward them. They got out of their car and jumped in a ditch, the mom covering her little girl.

When the tornado passed, they got up from the ditch and the mom asked the little girl, "Are you okay?"

The little girl replied, "Oh yes. Weren't they beautiful?"

The mom asked her what she was talking about and the girl replied, "Didn't you see how beautiful their wings were?"

The angels surrounded them in the middle of the tornado and the child saw the colored angel wings. Once again, the mom did not see them, only the child.

The pastor of a local church, across from the Joplin high school where people had gathered early for the evening services, upon hearing of the tornado, told everyone to go to the basement quickly. Once there, all four walls of the church fell to the basement, trapping the people underneath all the rubble when, they described six large men who appeared and lifted the four walls, allowing the survivors to climb out. When rescue squads arrived, and inquired as to how they got out, everyone had the same report.

Six big men lifted the walls up and allowed them to walk out and when everyone was out, they walked away saying they had others that they needed to help. All of them were descriptive and emphatic about the large men, telling the same story to the rescuers. The rescuers, in disbelief, explained there was no way six ordinary men could have lifted the four walls. There was one casualty at this location, though, but the rest were all miraculously saved. Can anyone say, "angelic intervention"?

One last story was the case of a family in their house with the tornado approaching. They all gathered together in the closet like they were often told to do, covering themselves with anything they could find. Suddenly, the roof was ripped off and the family started to pray. One of the children looked up and saw what he described as "butterfly people" hovering over the opening in the area above them. He said he could see the debris hitting them without any effect; they appeared to hover above them until the tornado had passed and the danger was gone. When they emerged, they could see the closet was the only room left standing.

This story was repeated several times, in different areas of the city, by different people of the city, who all claimed to see the "butterfly people" coming to their aid. There were also reports of people driving around and seeing people sitting on top of debris piles, crying over loved ones lost with what could only be described as a hooded figure that looked like the statues of angels in the cemetery standing behind them. Again, can anyone say, "angels"?

ANGELS, PAST, PRESENT, AND OCCASIONALLY HUMAN

Angels are not only servants of God, but they are also our fellow servants and are quick to not take any special position other than the ones they are appointed. I think the beginning of my interest must be attributed to the movie, "It's a Wonderful Life." In case you're not familiar with this holiday classic, the main character, George Bailey (played by Jimmy Stewart), owns a building and loan association that helps the everyday workingman buy a home that would otherwise be turned down by banks. George falls on hard times financially and gets to a point where he's contemplating suicide. Just as it gets almost to the point of no return, Clarence, his guardian angel, intervenes and shows George what life would have been like had he never been born and it's at this point he realizes all the good things he had done and how many lives he touched. He realizes he had a truly wonderful life and how it would have been a waste to throw it all away. This movie had a tremendous impact on me and showed me how angels are busy in our lives and are our helpmates and come to assist us in our time of need. Even though this motion picture was purely fiction, it's an excellent glimpse of how angels are involved in each one of our lives and I believe it to be true.

Not only do I believe we all have guardian angels, but it also appears churches have guardian angels as well. We see in Revelation 1, 2, and 3 John recording a vision of Jesus writing letters to the angels of the seven churches. He also referred to the angels as stars in 1:20. Angels do appear as human beings sometimes. *"There came two angels to Sodom at even; and Lot sat at the gate of Sodom; and Lot seeing them rose to meet them; and he bowed with his face toward the ground;"* (Genesis 19:1).

These same two angels also had the ability to strike blindness on those who sought to molest them. As the story goes, the Sodomites, upon realizing the angels were with Lot, came to the door and wanted them to come out so they could molest them. When Lot refused, they tried to force their way in. It was at this point the angels struck them with blindness. *"And they smote the men that were at the door of the house with blindness, both small and great: so that they wearied themselves to find the door."* (Genesis 19:11).

Angels also at least at one time had the ability to heal sickness.

> *Now there is in Jerusalem by the sheep market pool, which is in the Hebrew tongue called Bethesda, having five porches. in these lay a great multitude of impotent folk, of blind, halt, withered, waiting for the moving of the water: For an angel went at a certain season into the pool, and troubled the water: whosoever then first after the troubling of the water stepped in was made whole of whatsoever disease he had.* (John 5:2-4)

We also know from past reading that angels take on human characteristics, just like in the previous stories of the butterfly people. In Genesis, the Lord's angels came to Abraham on the planes of Mamre. *"And he took butter, and milk, and the calf which he had dressed, and set it before them: and he stood by them under tree, and they did eat"* (Genesis 18:8).

It appears *manna* is a regular staple of food for angels and is called angels' food. *"And had rained down manna upon them to eat, and had given them of the corn of heaven. man did eat angels food: he sent them meat to the full"* (Psalm 78:24-25).

We also know a jar of *manna* is one of the three items stored in the Ark of the Covenant, along with the tablets of the Ten Commandments and Aaron's rod. In the future, especially in the time of tribulation, we see in the book of Revelation angels are the most visibly active such as no time before. We read they have specific functions and duties that they are to carry out, such as the seven trumpets, the seven vials, and the seven seals. Angels are referred to as stars, as stated in Revelation 1. *"The mystery of the seven stars which thou sawest in my right hand, and the seven golden candlesticks. The seven stars are the angels of the seven churches: and the seven candlesticks which thou sawest are the seven churches"* (Revelation 1:20).

Recently, while preparing for a Bible study on the birth of Jesus, I came across an interesting observation. I read about the Magi and how they had met with King Herod and Herod had told them to go find the child that he, too, may worship him. Unknowing to them at the time, he had other plans in the works. The Scripture says, *"and when they heard the king, they departed: and lo, the star, which they saw in the east, went before them, and stood over where the young child was."* (Matthew 2:9). The phrase *"it stood over where the child was"* caught my attention. How could a star stand over where the child was? Could this have been an angel the Magi had seen? I find it hard to believe a star could stand over where the child was, but it would have been more logical for an angel to stand over him. I also believe sometimes when angels appear, they are a spectacular sight and even terrifying to some people, as in the case of the shepherds in the fields when they were told about the Lord's birth: *"And there were in the same country shepherds abiding in the field, keeping watch over their flocks by night. and lo, the angle of the Lord came upon them, and the glory of the Lord shone round about them: and they were sore afraid."* (Luke 2:8-9).

The shepherds being "sore afraid" tells me it was almost painful to behold this angel and was a terrifying sight, which is why I think most angels appear to people as people they may know or maybe a relative who has passed away. The reason for this is that it's more comforting to be around someone we are familiar with, rather than an angel appearing in all their glory, causing people to be "sore afraid."

At the time of this writing, I have a niece who was diagnosed with leukemia and is undergoing chemotherapy treatments and having a rough time. She tells her mother all the time that her grandmother, who passed away a few years ago, comes and visits her often and talks with her and even watches cartoons with her. I believe this is an angel who is there to comfort her. It is an example of how angels adapt to our situation so that it turns into a pleasant experience and not a terrifying one.

I also believe they speak to us in a voice that we are familiar with. Another perfect example of this was a case of this person I know (I'll withhold the name) who was sick and hospitalized. At the time of this writing, this person was not a Christian and ended up having an afterlife experience of which they saw a relative who had passed away a few years before. This angel appeared as a relative telling this person to go back, it wasn't their time yet. I believe this to be an angel taking the form of a familiar relative, telling this person to go back and get their life together, possibly saving this person from eternal damnation. I'm not sure what, if any, effect this experience had on this person, whether they took this as a warning and did what they needed to do to get saved or not, but it is a perfect example of an angel appearing as a relative to intervene on this person's behalf.

I recently heard of a story of policemen that came upon a car that had flipped over in a lake and was partially submerged. When they proceeded to make their way to the car, they heard a woman calling out to them to come and help them. When they got to the car, they found a woman and a small child. The woman was dead. The baby was unconscious and hanging upside down in her car seat. She had been there for about eighteen hours with no food or water in about forty-degree water and they couldn't explain where that voice came from, seeing there was just the two of them. All four policemen heard the voice. I believe this was an angel talking to them in a woman's voice, most likely the baby's mother.

At the time of this writing, my grandmother, who has reached the grand age of ninety-six and who lives with my aunt who takes care of her, says at night she can hear my grandmother on the monitor she has in her room. She is speaking to her mother, sister, and uncle. She said she saw a stairway made of gold and even stated her uncle was coming to get her. I can't think of anything other than angels speaking and appearing to her, comforting her. I can't help but think this vision of the stairway was the same vision my grandfather saw that I will explain later.

ANGELS AND DREAMS

I believe angels appear to us in dreams and Scripture supports this. In the story of the birth of Jesus, we see an example of angels appearing in dreams, warning Joseph to take the child Jesus and flee into Egypt: *"And when they were departed, behold, the angel of the Lord appeared to Joseph in a dream, saying, arise, and Take the young child and his mother, and flee into Egypt, and be thou there until I bring thee word: for Herod will seek the young child to destroy him.'"* (Matthew 2:13).

Again, after Herod's death, we see the angel appearing in a dream to tell Joseph to leave Egypt and go back to Israel. *"But when Herod was dead, behold, an angel of the Lord appeareth to Joseph in a dream in Egypt, saying, 'Arise,and take the young child and his mother, and go into the land of Israel: for they are dead which sought the young Child's life.'"* (Matthew 2:20).

God Himself also appears to people in dreams as we see in the story of Jesus' birth. The Magi had visited with King Herod and told him about the birth. Herod told them to go find him so that he can worship him too, but knowing his true intentions, God redirected their paths: *"And being warned in a dream of God that they should not return to Herod, they departed into their own country another way"* (Matthew 2:12).

I have on occasion had dreams of angels giving me messages and premonitions of things to come. On one occasion, right after I graduated from high school, my best friend had joined the navy and was stationed in Florida. One night, I had a dream that he came to me and told me he was going away.

Dreams being the way they are, I said, "I know you're in the navy. I already know you're away."

He said, "No, I'm here to tell you goodbye."

I asked, "What do you mean?"

He said, "When you wake up, you'll find out."

The next day, his mother called me to inform me that he had been killed in an automobile accident. In 2005, I had a dream about a terrorist attack in London, England and that it would involve bombs. I wasn't sure of the exact day, but it did happen on July 7th. There were a series of coordinating suicide attacks in central London. Four extremists separately detonated three bombs in quick succession aboard London underground trains across the city and later, a fourth on a double-decker bus.

My daughter, who is in her fourth year of dental school, told me that her grandparents (my mother and father-in-law) who had been dead for several years, came to her in a dream and told her how she had made them so proud.

In April of 2004, my sister passed away suddenly. My family and I were all in shock as she was only forty-eight years old. It was shortly after this time that I began to have a series of premonition dreams that are unexplainable. I can't explain the connection with my sister passing away and suddenly getting these dreams and still can't, but I had several dreams telling me of several major events that were to take place. Again, I didn't have any dates, but only the year.

I was told that there would be four hurricanes to strike the state of Florida. In the summer of 2004, for six weeks, Florida reeled under the assault of four hurricanes, first Charley struck Port Charlotte on August 13th, then Frances pounded Martin and Palm Beach, even collapsing part of Interstate 95. Next Ivan came ashore in Pensacola and the last of the four was Jeanne; it was known as "the year of the four hurricanes." It was told to me in a dream before it happened.

In another dream/premonition I had was that there would be a powerful earthquake in Indonesia and there would be a huge tsunami with massive loss of life. Once again, I didn't have an exact date, but only a year and it was the same year of 2004. As the year came to an end, I kind of sloughed off the dream about the earthquake and tsunami and thought maybe it wasn't going to happen and was relieved because I didn't want it to happen. It was the day after Christmas and I woke up when I heard the television in the other room. There was breaking news and I heard the newscasters talking of a major earthquake and tsunami. My mind went immediately to my dream and my only thought was, *Is it in Indonesia?* As I found out a few minutes later, it was exactly as my dream had revealed it to me.

There are a few dreams that have yet to materialize and I hope they never do. At the time of this writing, I dreamed there was a massive earthquake in the northwestern United States and that the Seattle/Tacoma, Washington area was devastated by an earthquake and a massive tsunami.

I'm not claiming to be able to tell the future or predict events, but all I know is periodically and for a brief time, I was informed of things that were going to happen. I haven't had any major dreams like this in a long time except for a few small things and I can't explain why it happened.

DEMONS

D emons are angels who made the choice to follow Lucifer, the archangel, in his insurrection against God along with the fallen angels, and they could be referred to as fallen angels also. Now the difference between fallen angels and demons is that it appears demons are spiritual and fallen angels are both physical and spiritual, as we saw in the Old Testament. The fallen angels (or giants as it's referred to in Genesis 6) physically came down to earth, whereas demons live in the air above the earth along with Satan.

There are three heavens: the first heaven is the space around us, the second heaven is where Satan reigns, and the third heaven is where the throne of God is. In Paul's epistle to the Corinthians, he states:

> *I knew a man in Christ above fourteen years ago, (whether in the body, I cannot tell; or whether out of the body, I cannot tell: God knoweth;) such a one caught up to the third heaven. And I knew such a man; (whether in the body, or out of the body, I cannot tell: God knoweth;) how that he was caught up into paradise, and heard unspeakable words, which it is not lawful for a man to utter. (2 Corinthians 12:2-4)*

The nature of demons is that they are evil; there are no good demons. They carry out the desires and orders of their master, Satan. They are intelligent and wise. They have knowledge and feelings. They are powerful, to the point that even God's angels in times past had trouble fighting them and had to call on assistance to over-come them. There's a story of at least one confrontation between Gabriel and the "prince of Persia," whom I understand to be an evil angel mentioned in the book of Daniel. Gabriel was sent to answer a prayer by Daniel to understand a vision he had been praying to understand. For twenty-one days, Daniel prayed to understand the vision, but Gabriel was unable to help him because the prince of Persia resisted him. So, Gabriel had to call for Michael to assist him in overcoming the obstacle, which was this demonic being who was preventing him from answering Daniel's prayer. It appears this skirmish took place for several days:

> *Then he said unto me, "Fear not, Daniel: for from the first day that thou didst set thine heart to under-stand, and to chasten thyself before thy God, thy words were heard, and I have come for thy words. But the prince of the kingdom of Persia withstood me one and twenty days: but, lo; Michael, one of the chief princes, came and helped me; and I remained there with the kings of Persia, now I have come to make thee understand what shall befall thy people in the latter days: for yet the vision is for many days."* (Daniel 10:12-14)

So, you see, even the angels have a tough time dealing with these evil spirits from time to time. So, in seeing this, we must realize we are no match with them in our own strength, but with heavenly assistance, we can overcome them.

A perfect example of humans trying to deal with demons in their own strength ended badly for a group of Jewish exorcists in the book of Acts. They tried to exorcise some demonic beings outside of the Spirit of God.

> *Then a certain of the vagabond Jews, exorcist, took*
> *upon them to call over them which had evil spirits*
> *the name of the Lord Jesus, saying, "We adjure you*
> *by Jesus whom Paul preacheth." And there were*
> *seven sons of one Sceva, a Jew, and chief of the*
> *priest, which did so. and the evil spirit answered*
> *and said, "Jesus I know, and Paul in know: but who*
> *are ye?" And the man in whom the evil spirit was*
> *leaped on them, and overcame, them and prevailed*
> *against them, so that they fled out of that house*
> *naked and wounded* (Acts 19:13-16).

Demons possess people from times past to even the present and are aware they are destined for damnation. Our Lord in His struggles against Satan and his demons cast out demons and cured those that were troubled by unclean spirits and who were demon possessed.

In the gospel of Mark, there's a story of Jesus encountering a man that was possessed with multiple demons. As the story goes, this man was terribly possessed and it says that when Jesus came upon him, the demons immediately recognized who Jesus was, which is common that demons know who Jesus is. Every time He came upon a person who was demon possessed, they immediately knew who He was. The demons recognized Him and acknowledged the fact that they were destined for damnation, but they also knew their time of torment was not yet to be as the Scripture records.

And when he (Jesus) *was come out of the ship, immediately there met him out of the tombs a man with an unclean spirit, who had his dwelling among the tombs;* (demons dwell among the dead) *and no man could bind him, no, not with chains* (He was extremely strong, another characteristic of a demon) *because he had been often bound with fetters and chains, and the chains had been plucked asunder by him, and the fetters broken in pieces: neither could any man tame him,* (He was totally out of control) *and always, night and day; he was in the mountains and in the tombs, crying and cutting himself with stones.* (Self-mutilation is a classic sign of demonic possession.) *but when he saw Jesus a far off, he ran and worshipped him,* (showing great fear) *and he cried with a loud voice, and said, "What have I to do with thee, Jesus thou son of the most high God? I adjure thee by God that thou torment me not."* (Recognizing the fact that Jesus has the power and will punish all ungodliness in the right time). (Mark 5 2-7)

In the previous chapter, I mentioned angels sometimes speak to people in a voice they are familiar with and, unfortunately, demons have the same ability to appear as something they are not. In 2 Corinthians, Paul admonishes Christians to be careful about this. And no *Marvel; for Satan himself is transformed into an angel of light.* (2 Corinthians 11:14). However, in 1 John, we are advised to try *"the spirits whether they are of God: because many false prophets have gone out into the world. hereby ye know the spirit God: every spirit that confesses that Jesus Christ has come in the flesh is of God: and every spirit that confesses not that Jesus Christ is come in the flesh is not of God: and this is the spirit of Anti-Christ,"* (1 John 4:1-3).

Now some people deny that demons exist and blame possessed people on mental illness, which in some cases might be true. However, we know for a fact that people can and are possessed. Christ spoke to demons that possessed people, which means they are real beings and not the result of some mental illness. The Lord has sealed believers and protects us from demonic possession, but the divine gift of free will does not prevent us from demonic possession. In other words, through curiosity and temptation, many believers and non-believers open themselves up for demonic possession, especially non-believers, through various channels such as the Ouija board, worldly pleasures such as drugs, excess alcohol, and others. This could explain why drug addicts display amazing supernatural strength when demons invade a human body. Now I'm not implying this means anyone who drinks alcohol or takes a pain-killing drug who has had surgery and so forth for that matter will become possessed by a demon, but I'm merely saying people open themselves up to these sorts of thing in large and excess amounts. I believe that's why many drug addicts that have overdosed often report seeing hallucinations and all sorts of fearful sights when they are under the influence of drugs in excess amounts. When demons invade a human body, they also produce blindness, insanity, suicidal thoughts, and muteness. The gospels state clearly that Jesus Christ believed in the reality of demons and His authority over them. Demons operate above the law of the natural realm; not only can they possess people, but they can also heavily influence and even control people without possessing them. They are unclean and violent. They conflict with Christians because Christ has given us power over them and they resent that. They are numerous and lack material substance and are invisible to the naked eye. However, as I have stated before, heavily drugged individuals, I believe, can and will see them.

We need not fear demons because as, I have said, Christ has given us power over them as John so eloquently stated in his first epistle: *"You, dear children are from God, little children and have overcome them: because greater is he that is in you, than he that is in the world"* (1 John 4:4).

> *"When thou passest through the waters, I will be with thee; and through the rivers, they shall not overflow thee: when thou walkest through the fire, thou shall not be burned; neither shall the flame kindle upon thee."* (Isaiah 43:2).

This verse was not only reassuring for divine protection, but it would also prove to be prophetic as we see in the book of Daniel. For those that have read the story about the three Hebrew children, Shadrach, Meshach, and Abednego, they had refused to obey the king's edict that all worship him as God, so the Babylonian king, Nebuchadnezzar, had them thrown into the fiery furnace. The book of Daniel says the fire was so hot that it consumed the men that were even at the door, but the three Hebrew children didn't even have the scent of smoke on their clothing, neither was their hair singed or their clothes burnt (see Daniel 3:20-27). We also know of the story of Daniel in the lion's den when the angel stayed the lions and saved Daniel from being eaten alive by them.

Growing up, I remember hearing stories of angelic interventions in my family, some occurring before I was born. My grandmother told me about my grandpa, who was killed in a refinery accident in Texas City, Texas in 1945, thirteen years before I was born. He lived for several days with third degree burns over ninety percent of his body. I remember my grandmother told me that on his last day right before he died, he told her that he could see the angels coming to get him on a ladder with a stairway with angels all around. He had two sisters who were devout Pentecostals—no makeup, no television, no radio, nothing but a piano in their house. There was a saying in our family that they had a direct line to God because there appeared to be some truth in it, as they would share with me angelic interventions in our family.

One such incident took place around January 1947. They lived in Texas City, Texas. When my Aunt Lolita (one of my grandpa's sisters) had a vision that she said was an angel who told her that they needed to pack up and move, as they were in danger. From whom or what, she wasn't told at the time. So, having faith as solid as a stone, she and her sister packed up everything they owned and moved to Seabrook, Texas, which is about twenty minutes down the road from Texas City. Just a few short months later, on April 16, 1947, the great Texas City disaster occurred, which to this day, is the largest man-made catastrophe in the United States. Nearly 600 people were killed, which includes the whole Texas City Fire Department and is the largest non-nuclear explosion to occur on American soil. My aunts were spared because of divine angelic intervention.

Another angelic intervention occurred even further back than that and had to do with the battle of San Jacinto. Horace Yeamans was my great-great-great-grandfather and was a veteran of the Texas-Mexico War. He had two brothers, Erastus and Elias Yeamans, who served under Colonel James Fannin and were subsequently massacred at Goliad. Upon hearing the news of this and the news of the Texians that perished at the Alamo, he and some others set out from their homes in Matagorda, Texas to travel by boat to San Jacinto with hopes of meeting up with General Sam Houston to fight against General Santa Anna. To do this, they had to travel up the Texas coast, through Galveston Bay and up what is now called the Houston ship channel to reach San Jacinto. When they reached Galveston Bay, they became stuck on a reef and were unable to free themselves. They remained there until long after the bullets stopped flying and the battle was over at San Jacinto.

This was angelic or divine intervention and it brought to my mind that when God allows a door to shut and won't allow you to go in, there's a good reason, for had he not been stalled on that reef and able to participate in the battle, there's was a chance he would have been killed and most of our family would not be here. so when God shuts a door for you, that's not always a bad thing. I am thankful to God for using a reef in Galveston Bay that assured not only the life of my ancestors to continue, but also for my very existence and my children and grandchildren.

One of my first experiences of having a guardian angel happened in the Gulf of Mexico one afternoon. My dad and I were fishing about five miles off the shore of Galveston. Everything was going fine. The fishing was good along with the weather and we had calm seas. After about six hours out on the water, I noticed the clouds starting to darken to our north. I asked my dad if he thought we should be heading back in. He didn't appear to be as concerned about it as I was; he was a hardheaded man. However, the wind and the seas started to pick up and it was then, when he decided we should start heading in, when I thought to myself that we should have done that a long time ago. By the time we pulled up anchor and started to head in, the wind and waves were larger and it started to look grave. By now, the wind had whipped up the waves to about twenty feet and being in a seventeen-foot boat was not a desirable position to be in.

My dad drove the boat and turned the bow into the waves. As the boat went up on a wave, it would be momentarily airborne and then would fall back down between the swells, only to be repeated. I thought I was going to die and remember saying to myself, *this is where my life ends,* and I was surely going to die. I had a lifejacket on and I knew I would be thrown out of the boat as it crashed into the waves and I would be lost at sea, never to be found. I was totally helpless and was about at the point I felt my life was over. Praying was the only option I had and it certainly couldn't hurt anything. So, I started praying for God to deliver us out of this dire situation and my prayer didn't go unanswered. After about fifteen minutes, there appeared a Coast Guard cutter alongside us. I felt a great comforting peace come over me. The Coast Guard didn't do anything as far as rescuing us, but just stayed beside us. It was comforting just to know they were there, in case things got worse. They followed us until we made it back into calmer waters. Once we were safe and I knew we would be okay, I turned around to wave as a sign of thank you to the guys on the Coast Guard ship but they were gone. I had no idea where they went and to this day, I can't explain where that Coast Guard cutter went and how it could get out of sight so quickly. There's no doubt in my mind it was a miracle.

WHEN THOUGH PASSETH THROUGH THE FIRE

I joined the Galveston Fire Department in October of 1979. I had only been on the job for four years when I experienced my first hurricane as a firefighter. I had been through a few hurricanes as a child, such as Hurricane Carla on September 11, 1961, which destroyed our house. Luckily, we evacuated against the wishes of my father who thought we could ride out the storm. Obviously, if we had stayed, we would not have survived, of which I attribute to divine intervention.

On August 17, 1983, Hurricane Alicia was bearing down on Galveston Island. We had responded to an apartment fire and upon arrival, we found a small apartment fire, which didn't take long to extinguish, but contending with hurricane-force winds, heavy rain, and flooding proved to be a real challenge for us. After the fire was out and we returned to our stations, I found myself on the rescue truck by myself because earlier, the decision was made to split up crews to have more apparatus responding to emergency calls for downed power lines and other things that may need our attention. Calls came in faster than we could answer them. As I left the scene of the fire, I found myself lost and alone on the seawall.

The seawall is exactly that, a seventeen-foot-high, seventeen-mile-long wall that was built after the great 1900 storm. To date, that was the worst natural disaster to strike the United States with a death toll of 8,000 people and destroyed the city of Galveston.

The seawall was designed to withstand the tidal surge, which is a surge of water the hurricanes push out ahead of the storm, kind of like a tidal wave. They vary with each hurricane and no one knows to this day how high the surge was that was generated by the 1900 storm. Some hurricane tidal surges have been as high as thirty-two feet, as was the case with Hurricane Camille on August 17, 1969.

As I made my way back, the rain came down so hard on the windshield I could not see. The report of traffic on the radio indicated there were tornadoes all around; I was terrified! It was then I realized I had lost my sense of direction and was not sure if the Gulf of Mexico was on my left or right. If I made the wrong turn, I could easily go over the seawall and be washed out to sea. I couldn't call on the radio because I wasn't sure where I was. So, I sat there for a few minutes. Suddenly, I could hear that voice — you know, the one you hear at the back of your head that suggests or tells you things that you hadn't thought of or had forgotten. I was "told" to turn my truck around with the back to the wind and rain so I could see at least a little better and sure enough, it worked! I could see the light poles on my right, so I knew I could turn right at the first street I came across and make my way back to the station. So, I turned right at the first street and finally I knew where I was. After dodging all kinds of debris and downed light poles, I eventually made my way back to the station. I was glad to see my coworkers and no longer felt like I was the last person on earth. I truly felt like divine intervention played a part in saving me from this dangerous situation.

In the next few days, I headed home or at least that was the plan. I wasn't sure if we even had a home to go to. Upon arriving at the apartment complex we lived in, I could see there was major damage everywhere. The roof was torn off in certain areas and on the ground. In the street, there were shingles and building materials everywhere and the first thought that came to my mind was, *Where are we going to live?* Expecting the worst, I went upstairs to our second-floor apartment, opened the door. Little did I know I was in for a huge surprise.

Everything was intact and exactly as we had left it. No water damage, no broken windows, or any other damage. It was as if nothing had happened at all. Our apartment was virtually untouched. If fact, our apartment was the only one that had a roof still intact. It looked as if someone had taken a saw and cut a straight line down each side of the roof. I remember the apartment manager telling me that I must be living right. I did pray before the storm, praying I would survive and our home would be spared. After some time, I sat in our apartment, exhausted, trying to rest the best I could with no air conditioning and no electricity, but we still had a home and I was thankful the Lord looked out for us.

Another incident I remember was when we responded to a structure fire at an old veterans' hospital that was under renovations. My engine company was the first to arrive. We saw heavy smoke coming out of the rear of the building on the top floor. Because the building was under renovations, the stairway was inaccessible; therefore, we had to wait for the two ladder trucks that had been dispatched to arrive. Upon arrival of the ladder trucks, one was placed at one end of the building where most of the heavy smoke was and where there was a window to gain access to the floor where we thought the fire was. The other was raised to the other end of the building. We had to stretch a hose line up the ladder to use once we gained access to the top floor. As I entered the window, I took a blind leap of faith that there was a floor there to catch me. As I think back now, this was a stupid thing to do. So, I jumped in the window and, thank God, there was a floor there, just a few feet below the window to catch me. Once again, I give credit to divine intervention. With my firefighter behind me and hose in hand, we proceeded to work our way to the other side, knocking fire down as we went. Unknown to me at the time, there was another engine company working their way to us. We eventually met up with them and informed the other captain that the fire behind us was out. The next job to do was to ventilate the area, which is to remove the heavy smoke that was trapped on the floor where the fire was that we just put out. This was the job of the other ladder truck. Ventilation of a building that had just undergone a fire is an extremely important part of firefighting and there's several reasons for this: it lowers the temperature, which enables firefighters to work more efficiently and it also increases visibility which enables the next phase of the fire extinguishment, which is called fire overhaul.

Simply put, that is the process that firefighters can seek out and find hidden hot spots that could erupt later, which is called a rekindle. As the smoke cleared and we could see more clearly, I was absolutely astonished to see that the floor we had just walked across had large gaping holes in them, whereas some merely extended to the next floor and some extended all the way down to the first floor, which was six floors down. I remember staring at the floor and then looking around trying to understand with my own eyes, but not saying a word about what just happened.

To add more elements to this story, there were several oxy-acetylene rigs used for welding that had survived the fire without exploding on us during the fire. I have no doubt this was a case of angelic intervention. I'm so thankful God's angels were there to protect me and those with me. *"The angel of the Lord encampeth round and bout them that fear him and delivereth them"* (Psalm 34:7).

In September of 2008, Hurricane Ike was bearing down on Galveston Island. It would be my fourth hurricane to experience working at the fire department. I was getting ready for work and as before, I knew I would probably be gone for days. So, I loaded up on food, clothes, water and other necessities to take with me. I saw my wife and daughter off for their evacuation, securing our house with the usual plywood over the windows and doors. However, this time I thought, *Why not anoint our house with olive oil?* It helped before and I was sure it would help again. It's a practice we have done in our church and other churches, anointing people with ailments and other physical needs.

When I got to work that morning, we were busy securing our fire station because we were to move farther into town. My station was in an area we call the west end of town. This is that part of Galveston that is not protected by the seawall. The upper administration decided we should stay at the San Luis Hotel, which is believed to be the highest point on the island from a flood standpoint. However, from the wind perspective, it wasn't such a safe location, as we would feel the full force of the hurricane winds, which were at the time around 120 miles per hour.

As the day went on, we answered medical calls concerning downed power lines and even a few small fires. About midday, I noticed the water level in the downtown was already about three feet. I called my wife and asked her the location of the hurricane, thinking it was close. She informed me it was still about 300 miles away. I remember thinking, *oh man, this is not good. The water is already this high and the storm is not even close. This is bad.* It was about this time we received a call of a large fire in a warehouse at the yacht basin, which is where people kept their boats for storage and where they keep them whenever they wanted to use them. Upon arrival, we found the warehouse to be completely involved and we were hampered by the high water and could not reach the building. The only option we had was to let it burn itself out and make sure the fire didn't involve any other buildings, but this wasn't the main problem. The main problem was a 100,000-gallon gasoline tank that was adjacent to the building. Gasoline floats on water and if that tank ruptured and the gasoline found its ignition source in the fire, that, combined with the flooding, that was downtown, could possibly set fire to the whole city and would be an ultimate catastrophe. This was a problem that was too big for us to handle and we would need help from Someone greater than ourselves. So, I remember thinking if the Lord didn't intervene, it would be a complete catastrophic event. We could not do anything about this situation and would have to totally rely on Him. This whole incident was in His hands and we were helpless. Whatever was going to happen was up to Him.

After a few hours, the fire burned itself out and there was no gasoline in the water and no other fires to deal with in this incident. It was many days later, as I reflected on it, that (1) I saw the problem, (2) realized it was beyond our control and we were helpless to do anything about it, (3) relied on the Lord to intervene, and (4) trusted Him who could and would handle it. So, the Lord intervened and I was amazed once again at His power and ability to solve a potential disaster from taking place. I think we as believers can apply these same steps to any problem we have in life because, let's face it, some of our problems are out of our control and all we can do is trust the Lord.

The rest of that night during the storm, we were stuck inside and could hear the horrific winds outside that could only be described as a thousand roaring lions and a sound you never forget. We lost power and running water after a few hours of being pinned inside. I could feel the whole building shaking. From the emergency lights that were activated when the lights went out, I could see the pictures on the wall shaking and thought they would fall at any moment. I remember thinking, *if there is a building collapse and we somehow survive, where would we go?* There was no place. As I thought of these things, fear set in, but it was soon replaced with peace; the peace that God gives you in times like these.

I remember it was about this time that my daughter called me, which was a miracle because I didn't think there was any service. The fear in her voice for me felt polarizing and she was more scared for me than I was for myself. I felt the peace the Lord gave me and told her everything was going to be fine and once this was all over, things would get back to normal. I was reminded with Scripture and comforting remembrances of what God had done for us in the past and He would surely come through for us again.

The next day, the devastation became a reality. As soon as the weather permitted, we went out to survey the damage. Hurricane Ike would no doubt be the worst hurricane in my lifetime and there was massive devastation. All the hurricanes I had experienced before were all wind events, meaning the damage done was mainly from the wind. This time, it was the floodwaters plus the wind. Everywhere we looked, there was damage. It appeared no house was untouched. It was sad to see houses that survived the flood-waters and the wind, only to catch fire because of the electricity being turned back on and exposed wires caught the houses on fire.

There was one subdivision where all the houses on the block were burned to the ground, so we had to bring in heavy equipment to bulldoze the remains into one pile. There was one lady who had been told her house survived the storm and she arrived to retrieve a few belongings. I'll never forget the look on her face when she saw her house had survived the storm, but didn't survive the fires.

She stood there for a while, crying. I didn't know what to say. It was one of those incidents when you ask why. Where was God? He came through on some miracles, but allowed other terrible things to happen. Why did He spare some things, but let other things take their course? It's one of those mysteries for which we simply don't have an answer.

This scene was to be repeated in the next several days. It was a real challenge as we did the house-to-house searches, looking for people, dead or alive. The nights were particularly bad as there were no lights and a deafening silence. The smell was awful and it felt like I was in a nightmare.

Being an island, which took a direct hit from this destructive hurricane, Galveston fared better that her neighbors to the East. The Bolivar Peninsula and a little seaside city called Crystal Beach were destroyed. There were only a few pilings where houses once stood. It looked like a giant bulldozer leveled the whole area.

When I finally got to go home, it was a challenge, as there were all kinds of debris in the road, including downed power poles, boats and cars that had been flipped. I had to drive through an obstacle course as I drove home. I was worried about our house and hoping everything would be okay and God would look out for us again like He did before. Seeing the debris in the road and the other destruction made my fears even greater. I live about fifteen miles north of Galveston and about a twenty-minute ride from the island. So, as I got closer to home, I noticed the mainland, as we call it, fared well compared to Galveston and Port Bolivar. As I turned down my street, there were a lot of tree branches and some metal from a carport that had come from somewhere. I pulled up to my house and had to physically remove tree branches and brush and a few pieces of wood and metal to even get close. I did a quick look outside and everything appeared to be in place on the outside. So, I made my way inside. I found no damage and, in fact, the lights were still on. Our house and a few others were the only ones to have electricity. To this day, I don't understand how this happened except it was a miracle. I was so grateful and knew God had watched over our home. I had to thank Him for His goodness.

77

The only damage, if you want to call it that, was a few missing shingles. Our detached garage didn't fare so well. Part of one wall was torn off, along with part of the roof. Ironically, a Christmas angel we had on a shelf hanging on the wall inside the garage wasn't touched in the slightest way. It was a little while later that I realized I had not anointed the garage or gave the garage much thought, being so concerned about the house. Yet, the main thing was God came through for us again. For us to have our house intact and to be one of the few houses in town to still have electricity was nothing short of a miracle.

ANGELS IN THE WILDERNESS

In the summer of 2013, my wife and I were in Big Sky, Montana. After a morning of fly-fishing, my wife had decided to take a nap. Being the restless one that I am, I decided to take a hike versus hanging out in the cabin. It was a beautiful day, not a cloud in the sky. The birds sang outside and everything was perfect. There was a nice little creek running through the property. It didn't take long to come across the first sign posted on a fence pole: "Warning: grizzly bear country. Be advised to carry bear spray at all times." I didn't think much of it. I enjoyed the beauty of the mountains, the stream, and all the sounds of nature.

I was about a few hundred yards from the cabin on the trail when I saw a squirrel on a tree branch. He looked at me, when suddenly, he started going crazy, making these strange noises. At first, I thought something was wrong with him, but then, it was as if someone had hit a switch and a deafening silence was all around me. It got so quiet that it practically hurt my ears. No bird sounds, no insects, nothing except for the squirrel sitting on the branch making frequent loud clicking sounds, as if panicking about something. I stood still for a few minutes. Then suddenly, I got an overwhelming feeling of danger and fear and all I could feel was the urgent need to leave the area immediately. I looked around, but it was as if the feeling grew more intense by the minute. I felt as though I were being watched, so I began to walk back to the cabin as fast as I could. The faster I walked, the more urgent the feeling was to get out of there. I felt as if something was behind me, chasing me. I kept looking back to see if there was anything following me, but there wasn't, as far as I could tell. So, I kept walking, eventually making it back to the cabin. Fearful and exhausted, I thought about what had happened and told my wife about it. After giving it some thought, I could only conclude that I was in danger of something on the trail and not sure what it was, but I have no doubt that it was divine intervention that caused me to flee the area.

The next day, my curiosity got the best of me and my wife and I went back to where the incident took place. As I looked around, there was a trail of padded down grass that had come down off the mountain, crossed the trail where I had previously stood and went down toward the creek. To this day, I'm not sure what came off that mountain and crossed the trail, but I know it was something dangerous and I was warned ahead of time to get out of there. Up until late July of 2016, my mysterious encounter in Montana was in the back of my mind that it was probably a bear encounter. Then one night, I was listening to coast-to-coast am radio show. Dave Paulides was the guest speaker, talking about strange disappearances in national parks and in his book and soon-to-be movie, *Missing 411*, he gives accounts of strange disappearances of hunters in the wilderness. He gives accounts of himself and other people having experienced the same thing I experienced in the woods and to this day remains a mystery. I emailed him and told him of my encounter and he told me that he didn't think it was a bear encounter and so the mystery remains.

CONCLUSION

There is much interest in angels today as ever and I think this is because as we near the end of the age, their activities will dramatically increase as evidenced in the book of Revelation. Security cameras have captured them on video and more and more stories are being reported of angelic interventions. The Bible tells us all we need to know about angels and as Christians, we must not only believe, but also depend on them for their strength and their gentleness. For their strength, such as rolling away the stone at the tomb of Jesus, destroying thousands in the Old Testament, we see how in the future, a single angel will bind Satan to the bottomless pit for a thousand years. We see Michael waging a war with Lucifer and his angels in the book of Revelation and casting them out of heaven. They administer God's judgment in the book of Revelation by way of the seven vials and the blowing of the seven trumpets. In our modern times, we saw examples of their strength in the stories of the butterfly people lifting the walls, holding back the tornado debris.

In their tenderness in ministering to Jesus in the Garden of Gethsemane, in announcing the birth of Jesus, encouraging us believers in our Christian walk, intervening at times on our behalf, and even rescuing us at times of need, they are our fellow servants and one day, we will be as they are. The only difference between them and us is they have not experienced the salvation issue like we have and our freedom to choose in everyday life between good and evil. We have choices every day and it is unclear whether they can fall today and choose evil, as did one-third that chose to align with Satan against God and rebel against the Most High. I tend to think not on this issue; however, they are just as active today as they have always been and will become even more active as we get closer to the end.

We are approaching the time when the heavenly angels will be more active than they have ever been before and those that are alive on the earth will witness the most angelic activity that has ever occurred in the history of man and creation. They have had to deal with Satan for eons and have had to watch his evilness, while he and his minions have destroyed, slandered, deceived, persecuted, murdered, and mocked the Lord and His people. They have been frustrated for a long time and I think the Lord will allow them to take their frustration out on the ungodly in the end time.

As I have mentioned in this book, they are our fellow servants and they serve the Lord and are at His command. If you ask most people if they believe in angels, most of them do, according to most polls, and a substantial portion of them have had angelic experiences. However, sadly, most people take them lightly and don't think about them until they are in desperate need and then they call on them. They are there to protect us and guide us every day. They are there when we wake up and they are there when we go to bed. They are there when we stumble and fall and to guide us back on the right track. Sometimes, they are absent for reasons unknown, but they are never far away. I've seen plenty of cases where there was no divine help, like the woman I mentioned that left her baby at home and died in a fire. I've seen automobile accidents where people were mangled and every bone in their body was broken. I've seen people with decapitations and amputated limbs. I remember this one incident where this man opened every gas jet in his house and then shot himself with a shotgun. It blew the whole house up. What could have driven him to do this?

As long as we remain here on earth, we will not know the answer to the question of why divine intervention is there and sometimes it's not. All we can do is trust the Lord for His divine protection. This protection is offered to all who want to have a relationship with our Heavenly Father. Besides Himself, the angels are the resources He offers to us. They can't be bought. They can't be earned. They are freely given, just like His love and salvation is to all who are willing to receive it. He accepts people just as they are, in any condition, and is willing to forgive them, no matter what they have done. For just as the word tells us, *"He is not willing that any should perish but have everlasting life"* (2 Peter 3:9). The *"spirit and the bride say, come. and let him that heareath say, come. and let him that is athirst say come. and whosoever will, let him take the water of life freely."* (Revelation 22:17).

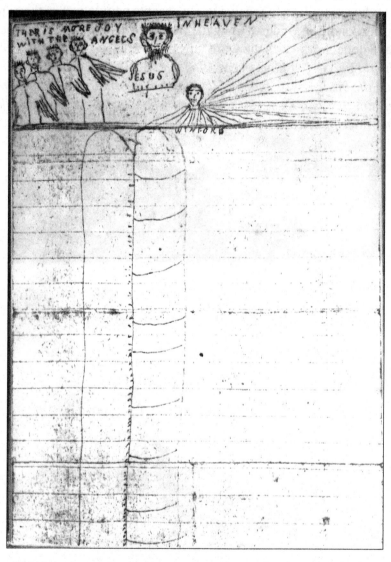

This is a picture of a drawing of the vision my grandpa saw of the angels on a ladder drawn by his dad (my great grandfather) mentioned on page 68

BIBLIOGRAPHY

King James Bible AMG international Inc, 1991

The Book- ofEnoch.com(2 v7), (7 v 11), (8 v 1)

World net daily article (hand of god sent missiles into sea) dated august 5· 2014

It's a Wonderful Life (movie) liberty films directed by Frank Capra

The book of giants the Gnostics library of the dead sea scrolls, 1Q 23 frag 1&6

The butterfly people of Joplin Missouri, was taken from article in abovetopsecret.com dated January 13, 2012

The Hagmann report.com on chimera article dated May 25· 2016.

The miracle of Dunkirk was largely taken from an article in Christians united .com dated May 5· 2010 by David Gardner.

ABOUT THE AUTHOR

Captain W.L. McLaren, Galveston Fire Department (retired), lives in Texas with his wife, Brenda, and their yellow Labrador Retriever, Bella. He and his wife are both active members of the Church of the Nazarene.

CPSIA information can be obtained
at www.ICGtesting.com
Printed in the USA
BVOW10s0327190717
489644BV00022B/315/P